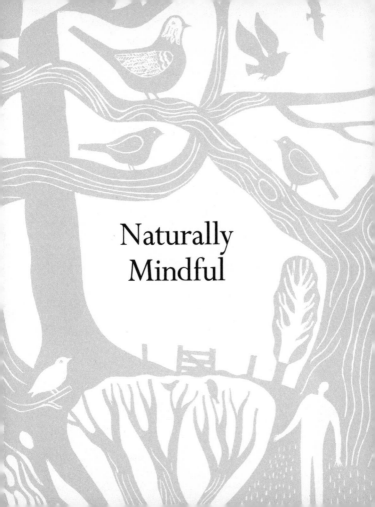

Naturally
Mindful

Naturally
Mindful

*Reconnecting with the Natural World,
Discovering Your True Self*

Leaping Hare Press

First published in the UK and North America in 2016 by

Leaping Hare Press

Ovest House, 58 West Street
Brighton BN1 2RA, UK
www.quartoknows.com

This book was conceived, designed and produced by

Leaping Hare Press

Publisher Susan Kelly
Creative Director Michael Whitehead
Editorial Director Tom Kitch
Art Director Wayne Blades
Series Commissioning Editor Monica Perdoni
Project Editor Fleur Jones
Designer Ginny Zeal
Illustrators Melvyn Evans, Clifford Harper,
Tessa Wardley & Sarah Young

British Library Cataloguing-in-Publication Data
A catalogue record for this book is available from
the British Library

ISBN: 978-1-78240-416-3

Printed in China

1 3 5 7 9 10 8 6 4 2

CONTENTS

Foreword 8

Introduction 12

CHAPTER ONE

Riding the Wave 18

CHAPTER TWO

Nature's Tonic 30

CHAPTER THREE

Unity 44

CHAPTER FOUR

Embracing Flux 58

CHAPTER FIVE

Travelling the Path 72

CHAPTER SIX

Immersion 88

CHAPTER SEVEN

Seeking Awareness 100

CHAPTER EIGHT

Nourishing the Self 108

CHAPTER NINE

Our True Nature 122

CHAPTER TEN

Living Mindfully 136

Directive 150
Notes 152
The Mindfulness Series 156
Index 158
Acknowledgements 160

Foreword

Nature is around us and within us always. How would we be here, experiencing life, if it weren't for our bodies, air, water, trees, birds, the sun and the sky? The simple answer is that we wouldn't. Nature gives rise to all life, including our own. Our bodies and minds originated in the natural world and are made up of nature's elements. We are nature and part of something much greater than ourselves: the wonderful, awe-inspiring web of life.

❧ But we have forgotten this undeniable truth and live our lives as if we were separate from nature. With the evolution of the wonderfully creative human mind and our incredible ability for conscious abstract thought, we spend more time dreaming

up theories, concepts and belief systems than paying attention to our direct experience. Simultaneously, our lives have become increasingly urban and spent indoors. Neglecting our innate bond with nature is the cause of much of the suffering in our world — in fact, 'nature deficit disorder' is contributing to an epidemic of unhappiness and the current global environmental crisis.

So what has mindfulness to do with all this? Mindfulness is paying attention, without judgement and with kindly curiosity, to the unfolding of our experience moment by moment. It is appreciating life within us and around us. It is really experiencing life. This ancient Buddhist practice, which originated thousands of years ago, has never been more relevant to making our planet a better place.

🦢 It's time, then, to bring our awareness back to the natural world. Why? Firstly, experiencing nature will make us happier — science has proved it vital for our health and wellbeing. Secondly, practising mindfulness in nature will make us wiser. The natural world holds one of life's greatest truths — that our wellbeing is intimately linked with that of the rest of nature, so what we do to the rest of nature, we do to ourselves. This leads us to the third reason to restore our innate bond with the natural world: it is essential if we are to address the current environmental crisis.

🦢 People protect what they love and a true love of nature will inspire solutions to the creation of a more sustainable world. My belief is that everyone can fall in love with nature — because we are nature.

We just need to (re)discover our favourite ways of enjoying nature – mindfully, of course. Let this little book inspire you to experience the natural world, to love it, share it and care for it with all your heart. It's time to celebrate the wonderful, mysterious, unfathomable opportunity we have all been gifted with: life.

CLAIRE THOMPSON Author of *Mindfulness & the Natural World* and *The Art of Mindful Birdwatching*

INTRODUCTION

You lie on your back in a green field; you feel the sun on your skin, you feel the bones of the earth supporting your bones; you slide your fingers through the short, squeaky grass, feeling its tough stalkiness, maybe gently bruising some scent out of it. Far away, so barely visible that you have to focus hard, you can see a tiny bird spiralling up into the sky, singing a song you can hardly hear. When it reaches the top of its ascent it hangs there, singing its joyful finale. Everything around you is suspended. You find you are relaxed and aware at the same time, connecting with the world through sight, sound, touch and scent – and all you had to do was lie down and still your mind. You have discovered natural mindfulness.

🐦 Paradoxically, for some of us, fitting mindfulness into our lives can be as stressful as the problems we are trying to resolve. We sometimes dread the ten-minute mindfulness session we have booked in with ourselves as much as the gym session we know will be good for us but has just become another chore. It's possible to become slaves to the mindfulness version of the fitband, which means you are focusing on the result, not the process. The aim, surely, is to make mindfulness an everyday, natural thing. If you are new to mindfulness techniques, you may feel a bit pressured, trying to 'be mindful' in the middle of a busy office, or missing the special times of the day you've earmarked for a session. If you have some mindfulness mileage under your belt, you will recognize the feeling of something just going a bit stale – like the once-energizing exercise routine that

now leaves you flat. If this sounds familiar, check in with yourself – do you feel you are just going through the mindfulness motions? Mindfulness is not about box-ticking. Sometimes you just need a reboot.

🐦 Luckily, the solution is simple. Get out. Get back to nature. Instead of trying so hard to find mindfulness in the whirling world, look to the natural world. Give yourself a break from the treadmill (literal and metaphorical) and go for a walk. Leave your earplugs behind, and switch off your phone. Fresh air and sunshine bring physical benefits that we all know about. Everyone feels in possession of a clearer mind after a 25-minute walk – and it is important that you walk, don't run or jog. Aim to walk slowly enough to observe the world. Take time to look up; give yourself space to stop and stare.

The natural world is an endless source of discovery that is free and accessible to us at all times.

From 'MINDFULNESS & THE NATURAL WORLD'
CLAIRE THOMPSON

❧ Get out into the countryside or a park. Open yourself and your senses to the elements. Let the wind push you, stare at the sky, look under stones for tiny worlds. Tune in to the birdsong, without worrying which bird it is; find a tree that you love and visit it throughout the seasons, focusing on its slow changes. Spend time by a stream, watching the sunbeams glance off the mini whirlpools. Dip your hands in the cold of the water; stand still enough so that the fish ignore you and show themselves.

❧ Never neglect the chance to still your mind in a garden; gardens have always been a backdrop to mindful communication with nature. Enthrall yourself in a rose; concentrate on a small patch of dappled light; let your mind sink into the green all around you.

ॐ Always make time for the sea. Water encourages meditation, and the sea, the mother of us all, offers a masterclass in mindfulness. It's always the same, yet constantly changing: a living meditation. Listen to the seabirds, the suck and sigh of water on sand or pebbles; smell the salt spray; look at the changing colours, constant and moving. Let yourself be rocked into mindfulness the natural way.

ॐ Mindfulness should come naturally. Children can do it – how did we lose the knack? Nature can help us rediscover it. To give you a helping hand, *Naturally Mindful* offers a harvest of quotes, inspirations, insights and mantras on the natural theme from a collective of expert authors. Take it with you on your next walk, to get you started. Let nature keep you mindful, and be mindful of nature.

CHAPTER ONE

RIDING THE WAVE

WATER IS THE ESSENCE OF
LIFE, AND EVEN RAINDROPS ON A
WINDOWPANE ENCOURAGE US TO
ENGAGE IN MINDFULNESS PRACTICE. BUT
WHEN YOU HAVE THE OPPORTUNITY,
HEAD FOR THE SEA – IT COMMANDS
ATTENTION, IN ALL ITS MOODS.

ADAPTING

Surfing brings you face to face with the raw beauty of nature at different volumes and tones, and in this setting there is the opportunity to be mindful not by moving inwards to the self but by adapting to what the environment affords.

From 'MINDFULNESS & SURFING'
SAM BLEAKLEY

WATER

—————————◆—————————

Water is the driving force
of all nature.

LEONARDO DA VINCI
RENAISSANCE ARTIST AND INVENTOR (1452–1519)

TAKING OFF

◆

*I have sensed the sudden suspension
of time — sought by all meditative techniques —
deep inside the 'tube'; and been clipped by that
same wave then dragged across a razor-sharp
live coral reef as the water curtain falls to
the sea god's applause.*

From 'MINDFULNESS & SURFING'
SAM BLEAKLEY

22

HERE & NOW

◆

*Trying to push negative thoughts
away only causes us to get tangled up in them
further. In contrast, consider how you feel about
raindrops when you watch them gently spatter
a windowpane. That's acceptance.*

From 'MINDFULNESS & THE BIG QUESTIONS'
BEN IRVINE

THE SEA

◆

The sea possesses a power over
one's moods that has the effect of a will.
The sea can hypnotize.

From 'THE LADY FROM THE SEA'
HENRIK IBSEN
NORWEGIAN PLAYWRIGHT AND POET (1828–1906)

OCEAN HEALING

♦

*Mindfulness in surfing is,
paradoxically, a moving out of mind into the
world, moving against the grain of inner-directed
thought and reflection into an acute sense of
what the environment demands of us — where
winds, currents, beach shapes, wave types
and lunar-tidal movements meet.*

From 'MINDFULNESS & SURFING'
SAM BLEAKLEY

ONE DROP

◆

*One drop of water helps to swell
the ocean; a spark of fire helps to give
light to the world. None are too small,
too feeble, too poor to be of service.
Think of this and act.*

HANNAH MORE
ENGLISH WRITER (1745-1833)

BREAKING FREE

◆

*The wave rises, light and crisp,
breaking free from the anchor that is the
deep swell, the incessant tidal motion,
the undercurrent, the pulse. Waves
are a delicate presence woven
into the sea's force.*

From 'MINDFULNESS & SURFING'
SAM BLEAKLEY

THE MINDFUL LIFE

◆

We can liken our minds to the ocean.
There are waves on the surface, always moving,
never really still; this is the level of thought.
But there are also the depths of the ocean,
with all its power and beauty. The depths
are still and rich with life.

From 'MINDFULNESS & COMPASSION'
THE HAPPY BUDDHA

LIFE STIRRING

*The sea is everything. It covers seven
tenths of the terrestrial globe. Its breath is
pure and healthy. It is an immense desert,
where man is never lonely, for he feels
life stirring on all sides.*

From 'TWENTY THOUSAND LEAGUES UNDER THE SEA'
JULES VERNE
FRENCH NOVELIST, POET AND PLAYWRIGHT (1828–1905)

CHAPTER TWO

NATURE'S TONIC

TO KNOW NATURE IS TO UNDERSTAND IT,
AND TO UNDERSTAND IT IS TO LOVE IT.
WHEN YOUR SOUL IS IN NEED OF A TONIC,
SPEND TIME IN NATURE AND DISCOVER
FOR YOURSELF ITS GENEROSITY.

FREEDOM

*Children ... find their freedom in
Nature by being able to love it. For love is
freedom: it gives us that fullness of existence
which saves us from paying with our soul for
objects that are immensely cheap. Love lights up
this world with its meaning and makes life
feel that it has everywhere that 'enough'
which truly is its 'feast'.*

From 'THE RELIGION OF MAN'
RABINDRANATH TAGORE
INDIAN POET (1861–1941)

UNCONDITIONAL LOVE

Nature is kind, compassionate and generous; she is filled with unconditional love. From a tiny seed grows a great apple tree that produces thousands upon thousands of apples, year after year.

From 'SOIL, SOUL, SOCIETY'
SATISH KUMAR

LANDSCAPE DRAWING

◆

Like all mindful drawing,
drawing landscapes needs to start with seeing.
So find a spot in nature that appeals to you
and take some time to sit and see it.

From 'MINDFULNESS & THE ART OF DRAWING'
WENDY ANN GREENHALGH

WE HAVE ENOUGH

*Nature provides enough for
everybody's need but not enough
for even one person's greed.*

MAHATMA GANDHI
INDIAN INDEPENDENCE LEADER AND LAWYER (1869–1948)

Pure Awareness

◆

*The immanence of nature draws out
a sense of transcendence in even the most
earthbound of us, and for many it has a spiritual
aspect that goes beyond words or theologies.
It grounds us in our own being, and with
the energy and atmosphere of the
natural world.*

From 'MINDFULNESS & THE ART OF DRAWING'
WENDY ANN GREENHALGH

CREATIVITY & CALM

*Immersion in nature has an
immediate impact. It releases the playful
child inside, stimulates our senses and awakens
our wonder. This, in turn, shifts our attention
and makes room for creativity and calm
to come to the fore.*

From 'MINDFULNESS & SURFING'
SAM BLEAKLEY

LOOKING DEEP

◆

Look deep into Nature, and then you

will understand everything better.

ALBERT EINSTEIN
GERMAN-BORN PHYSICIST (1879–1955)

ENDING THE TYRANNY OF THOUGHTS

---

*A silent mind is alive; it is clear
and unclouded by fear and craving.*

From 'MINDFULNESS & COMPASSION'
THE HAPPY BUDDHA

In the Midst of Nature

There can be no very black melancholy

to him who lives in the midst of Nature

and has his senses still.

From 'WALDEN'
HENRY DAVID THOREAU
AMERICAN PHILOSPHER, JOURNALIST AND POET (1817–62)

GOOD WEATHER

Sunshine is delicious, rain is refreshing,
wind braces us up, snow is exhilarating;
there is really no such thing as bad weather,
only different kinds of good weather.

JOHN RUSKIN
ENGLISH ART CRITIC (1819–1900)

CONTENTMENT

◆

He is richest who is content with the least,

for content is the wealth of nature.

SOCRATES
GREEK PHILOSOPHER (c. 470–399 BCE)

LEARNING FROM NATURE

◆

*To understand nature we
have to experience nature, we have to be
in nature and we have to learn from nature,
rather than learning about nature.*

From 'SOIL, SOUL, SOCIETY'
SATISH KUMAR

‿

CHAPTER THREE

UNITY

AT THE HEART OF ALL SPIRITUAL
TRADITIONS IS THE BELIEF THAT WE ARE
ONE WITH ALL THINGS AND ALL BEINGS.
SPENDING TIME IN NATURE HELPS
US TO APPRECIATE THIS UNITY.

WE ARE NATURE

*All plants, animals and minerals
are nature. They do not separate themselves
from one another. They simply co-exist.
We are the same. We are an integral part
of the natural world.*

From 'MINDFULNESS & THE NATURAL WORLD'
CLAIRE THOMPSON

HARMONY

◆

Love and reverence for the Earth will automatically result in sustainability, coherence and harmony.

From 'SOIL, SOUL, SOCIETY'
SATISH KUMAR

The Sounds of Life

---

*Our voices connect us with the rest of
the natural world, and we honour that sacred
connection most when we use them to sing.*

From 'THE ART OF MINDFUL SINGING'
JEREMY DION

ONE WITH NATURE

*One touch of nature makes
the whole world kin.*

From 'TROILUS AND CRESSIDA'
WILLIAM SHAKESPEARE
ENGLISH PLAYWRIGHT AND POET (1564–1616)

SHARING MOMENTS

Mindful birdwatching is sharing a unique moment in space and time with another animal. It is being with the bird rather than simply looking at, hearing or identifying it.

From 'THE ART OF MINDFUL BIRDWATCHING'
CLAIRE THOMPSON

EMPATHY

Be mindful in your personal actions and act with empathy and compassion towards the environment and others.

From 'THE MINDFUL ART OF WILD SWIMMING'
TESSA WARDLEY

FREEING OURSELVES

*A human being is a part of the whole,
called by us 'Universe', a part limited in
time and space. This delusion is a kind of
prison for us ... Our task must be to
free ourselves from this prison by
widening our circle of compassion to
embrace all living creatures and
the whole nature in its beauty.*

ALBERT EINSTEIN
GERMAN-BORN PHYSICIST (1879–1955)

ABUNDANCE

---◆---

To live a pure unselfish life, one must

count nothing as one's own in the

midst of abundance.

THE BUDDHA
(c. SIXTH CENTURY BCE)

WE ARE ALL RELATED

*What we do to nature we do to ourselves.
If we harm nature, we harm ourselves. We are all
related; we live in an interdependent world.*

From 'SOIL, SOUL, SOCIETY'
SATISH KUMAR

THE TREE

◆

Emancipation from the bondage of
the soil is no freedom for the tree.

From 'FIREFLIES'
RABINDRANATH TAGORE
INDIAN POET (1861–1941)

EVERYTHING CONNECTS

In nature we never see anything isolated,
but everything in connection with something else
which is before it, beside it, under it and over it.

JOHANN WOLFGANG VON GOETHE
GERMAN WRITER AND STATESMAN (1749–1832)

Bound Together

◆

Humankind has not woven the web of life.
We are but one thread within it. Whatever we do
to the web, we do to ourselves. All things are
bound together. All things connect.

ATTRIBUTED TO CHIEF SEATTLE
NATIVE AMERICAN CHIEF (1786–1866)

CHAPTER FOUR

EMBRACING FLUX

TO TRY TO CONTROL LIFE IS TO
BE IN CONFLICT WITH IT; TO GO WITH
THE FLOW IS TO BE IN HARMONY WITH IT.
MINDFULNESS PRACTICE HELPS US TO
EMBRACE FLUX AS NATURE DOES.

CHOICELESS AWARENESS

◆

The natural way is for all things to

arise and to pass away.

From 'MINDFULNESS & COMPASSION'
THE HAPPY BUDDHA

LIFE FLOWS

◆

Nothing that is can pause or stay;

The moon will wax, the moon will wane,

The mist and cloud will turn to rain,

The rain to mist and cloud again,

Tomorrow be today.

From 'KÉRAMOS'
HENRY WADSWORTH LONGFELLOW
AMERICAN POET (1807–82)

FISH & BIRD

◆

Surfers must inhabit a thin line between fish and bird at the ocean's skin, and bust out their carnival moves as the thunder of sets rolls by.

From 'MINDFULNESS & SURFING'
SAM BLEAKLEY

PATIENCE

◆

Trying to change your mind wilfully is like trying to change the weather — impossible.

From '**MINDFULNESS & COMPASSION**'
THE HAPPY BUDDHA

YIN & YANG

—————————— ◆ ——————————

Water's motion is the flux of the Tao —
the forgiving yin against the fearless yang.
'Highest good is like water', wrote the Chinese
philosopher Lao Tzu. 'It comes
close to the Way.'

From '**MINDFULNESS & SURFING**'
SAM BLEAKLEY

EBBING & FLOWING

Relax into the flow and notice how your breathing becomes one with your movements, ebbing and flowing with the rhythm of the waves.

From 'THE MINDFUL ART OF WILD SWIMMING'
TESSA WARDLEY

A CONSTANT LESSON

◆

On each occasion of bliss and fear,
I am educated into the complex ways of the
sea — a constant lesson in mindfulness.

From 'MINDFULNESS & SURFING'
SAM BLEAKLEY

What's the Weather Like?

◆

*Weather terms are a rich source of
language for describing emotions — calm,
unsettled, dull, bright and turbulent. Finding
a word to describe the 'weather inside' lends a
degree of objectivity to your experience.*

From 'MINDFULNESS FOR UNRAVELLING ANXIETY'
RICHARD GILPIN

LIVING LIFE BACKWARDS

◆

In Zen, there is a 'reverse' law. When you try to float on water you sink, and when you try to sink you float. You need very little effort to stay afloat — simply fill your lungs with air. Easy, really.

From 'MINDFULNESS & COMPASSION'
THE HAPPY BUDDHA

SOUND & SILENCE

We can never seek silence on its own without sound; in the natural world, sound and silence come together.

From 'THE ART OF MINDFUL SILENCE'
ADAM FORD

LETTING GO

◆

For after all, the best thing one can do

When it is raining, is to let it rain.

From 'THE BIRDS OF KILLINGWORTH'
HENRY WADSWORTH LONGFELLOW
AMERICAN POET (1807–82)

Spontaneous Change

◆

Life is a series of natural and
spontaneous changes. Don't resist them;
that only creates sorrow. Let reality be reality.
Let things flow naturally forward in
whatever way they like.

LAO TZU
CHINESE PHILOSPHER AND POET (c. SIXTH CENTURY BCE)

∽

CHAPTER FIVE

TRAVELLING THE PATH

AS YOU TRAVEL ALONG THE
EXHILARATING, CHALLENGING PATH
THAT IS LIFE, REMEMBER THAT THE WORLD
IS A GIFT. TAKE EACH MOMENT AS IT IS,
WITHOUT JUDGEMENT – BUT DO TAKE
IT, AND RELISH THE TRANSITION.

Venturing Out

◆

Above all, do not lose your desire to walk: every day I walk myself into a state of wellbeing and walk away from every illness; I have walked myself into my best thoughts, and I know of no thought so burdensome that one cannot walk away from it.

SØREN KIERKEGAARD
DANISH PHILOSOPHER (1813–55)

THE SOLO SWIM

---

*How you manage a swim on your own
is up to you. Be bold, but thoughtful; take on
the adventure but be aware of your limits.
Relish the decisions to be made and focus on
every stroke of your journey.*

From 'THE MINDFUL ART OF WILD SWIMMING'
TESSA WARDLEY

TRUE PLACES

---◆---

It is not down in any map; true places never are.

From 'MOBY-DICK'
HERMAN MELVILLE
AMERICAN NOVELIST AND POET (1819–91)

COMPASSION

◆

Compassion is not only a feeling of warmth

or acceptance, it is an understanding

that this moment is as it is.

From 'MINDFULNESS & COMPASSION'
THE HAPPY BUDDHA

FIND A PLACE

We do not have to go far to find a place
where we can find silence in nature.

From 'THE ART OF MINDFUL SILENCE'
ADAM FORD

CALL OF THE WILD

◆

The world does not set out to control us,
it merely presents itself in all
its glory and moods.

From 'MINDFULNESS & SURFING'
SAM BLEAKLEY

STEPPING INTO THE RIVER

---◆---

No man ever steps in the same river twice,

for it's not the same river and he's

not the same man.

HERACLITUS OF EPHESUS
GREEK PHILOSOPHER (c. SIXTH CENTURY BCE)

PILGRIMAGE

There is pleasure in the pathless woods,

There is a rapture on the lonely shore,

From 'CHILDE HAROLD'
LORD BYRON
ENGLISH POET (1788–1824)

TAKING IN THE VIEW

◆

*Judgement cramps the mind, making life
into a chilly, inhospitable affair.*

From 'MINDFULNESS FOR UNRAVELLING ANXIETY'
RICHARD GILPIN

The Road to Truth

◆

There are only two mistakes one can make

along the road to truth: not going

all the way, and not starting.

THE BUDDHA
(c. SIXTH CENTURY BCE)

MAKE IT MINDFUL

◆

*Reaching the water is all part
of the experience. Make it mindful. Take
a moment to enjoy the transition.*

From 'THE MINDFUL ART OF WILD SWIMMING'
TESSA WARDLEY

REPLENISHING WHAT
WE HAVE TAKEN

◆

According to the principle of yagna,
we should celebrate the beauty, the abundance and
the grandeur of nature by replenishing what we
have taken. If we take five trees to build our home,
we must replenish them by planting fifty trees.

From 'SOIL, SOUL, SOCIETY'
SATISH KUMAR

GIFT

The world is a gift, not a commodity.

From 'MINDFULNESS & SURFING'
SAM BLEAKLEY

IMMENSE SILENCE

*Great rocks have their own weight
and silent presence, resting, perhaps for
many millennia, in one spot. The gravity
of their silence is immense.*

From 'THE ART OF MINDFUL SILENCE'
ADAM FORD

CHAPTER SIX

IMMERSION

LIVING MINDFULLY IS ABOUT
IMMERSING YOURSELF TOTALLY IN THE
MOMENT, WHATEVER ACTIVITY YOU ARE
ARE ENGAGED IN – SWIMMING, SURFING,
SINGING, DRAWING OR SIMPLY BEING
SILENT IN NATURE.

PRESSING PAUSE

Imagine time slowing down,
so that you're unaware of it passing.
Imagine timelessness, a pause in the spinning
of the world, where a few minutes might feel
like an hour, or an hour like a few minutes.

From 'MINDFULNESS & THE ART OF DRAWING'
WENDY ANN GREENHALGH

ECO OVER EGO

Never immerse in yourself — that is the ego at work; always immerse in the environment, letting the eco take off and take over.

From 'MINDFULNESS & SURFING'
SAM BLEAKLEY

STEP INTO THE UNKNOWN

———◆———

Relish your feelings of fear and excitement.
Don't fight them; acknowledge them but don't be
controlled by them. Take a deep breath, hold your
chin up high and take a step into the unknown.

From 'THE MINDFUL ART OF WILD SWIMMING'
TESSA WARDLEY

Engage Your Senses

◆

Smell, watch, touch, taste, listen to
nature as often as you can. We can all discover
how much life we hold in us that way.

From 'MINDFULNESS & THE NATURAL WORLD'
CLAIRE THOMPSON

LIFE-CENTRED

*To truly care for our world, we must
move from a self-centred to a life-centred mode
of existence, and this is what mindfulness
is all about.*

From 'MINDFULNESS & COMPASSION'
THE HAPPY BUDDHA

BODYMINDFULNESS

◆

Stay focused on the sounds, smells and tastes of the environment and allow them to shape your experience. 'Bodymindfulness' is not being in your mind, but being present in the environment.

From 'MINDFULNESS & SURFING'
SAM BLEAKLEY

TOUCHING SILENCE

Discover what silence can do for you.

From 'MINDFULNESS & THE ART OF DRAWING'
WENDY ANN GREENHALGH

REFLECTIONS

Mindfulness is a within-body reflection
as well as a within-mind reflection.

From 'MINDFULNESS & SURFING'
SAM BLEAKLEY

NOTICING

Notice your breathing: inhale, exhale, relax.

From 'MINDFULNESS AT WORK'
MARIA ARPA

YOUR SACRED VOICE

Everything in the known universe is singing, and your voice is your sacred contribution to the grandest of orchestras.

From 'THE ART OF MINDFUL SINGING'
JEREMY DION

CHAPTER SEVEN

SEEKING AWARENESS

SOMETIMES, WITHOUT EVEN
THINKING ABOUT IT, WE HAVE A
FLEETING SENSE OF BEING AT ONE WITH
THE WORLD – A SENSE OF AWAKENING.
PRACTISING MINDFULNESS ALLOWS
US TO SEEK OUT AND INVITE THOSE
MOMENTS CONSCIOUSLY
INTO OUR LIVES.

BALANCE

The point of complete identification
of mind with body, where the mind is absorbed
by and continuous with the balance of the body,
is surely what Buddhists describe as
bodhi *or 'awakening'.*

From 'MINDFULNESS & SURFING'
SAM BLEAKLEY

PRESENCE

---◆---

Mesmerized into a gentle trance by watching the gulls in flight, I was struck by their extraordinary presence and awareness, completely at one with the sea breeze.

From 'THE ART OF MINDFUL BIRDWATCHING'
CLAIRE THOMPSON

TAKING ATTENTION
OUT OF THINKING

◆

Lengthen the out-breath by a second or two.

This works because to lengthen the out-breath we

need to give our attention to it — which means

we must take our attention out

of our thinking.

From 'MINDFULNESS & COMPASSION'
THE HAPPY BUDDHA

BEING SHAPED

◆

*To 'perform' surfing is a first step,
to 'think with' surfing is a second step, to let
surfing think you and perform you or to be
shaped by the total environment that we
conveniently reduce to the act of 'surfing'
is a more expansive step still.*

From 'MINDFULNESS & SURFING'
SAM BLEAKLEY

SOARING

Who has never stopped to gaze longingly at a bird soaring effortlessly through the sky?

From 'THE ART OF MINDFUL BIRDWATCHING'
CLAIRE THOMPSON

THE ABSENCE OF THINGS

The sky exists, but it is not a thing in itself —
it is the absence of things, but yet it exists. You
cannot grab the sky and put it in your pocket,
nor can you bottle it, but it's there.

From 'MINDFULNESS & COMPASSION'
THE HAPPY BUDDHA

CHAPTER EIGHT

Nourishing the Self

WE ARE ENCOURAGED TO
LOOK AFTER OTHERS, BUT IT IS JUST AS
IMPORTANT TO LOOK AFTER OURSELVES.
CONTEMPLATING THE STILLNESS OF THE
NATURAL WORLD IS THE IDEAL WAY TO
GAIN PESPECTIVE IN OUR LIVES.

HEALING

◆

I go to nature to be soothed and healed,

and to have my senses put in tune once more.

From 'THE GOSPEL OF NATURE'
JOHN BURROUGHS
AMERICAN NATURALIST (1837–1921)

OUR NATURAL HOME

*The natural world — our natural home —
is a great source of silence, if by silence
we mean neither talking to other people
nor being talked to.*

From 'THE ART OF MINDFUL SILENCE'
ADAM FORD

TAKING THE PLUNGE

---❖---

Water is calming, inspiring, and brings
us peace; take the plunge and immerse yourself
in the health-giving waters.

From 'THE MINDFUL ART OF WILD SWIMMING'
TESSA WARDLEY

BEAUTY

---◆---

To the artist there is never

anything ugly in nature.

AUGUSTE RODIN
FRENCH SCULPTOR (1840–1917)

VISUALIZING

Visualize before you act. You can paddle out,
catch and surf a wave in your mind's eye,
but the secret is to not stay in the mind's eye,
but to visualize a whole bodily change.

From 'MINDFULNESS & SURFING'
SAM BLEAKLEY

FINDING HUMILITY

The challenge for humankind, in the twenty-first century, is to find humility and reconnect with nature.

From 'SOIL, SOUL, SOCIETY'
SATISH KUMAR

Here & Now

---◆---

Our worst misfortunes never happen,

and most miseries lie in anticipation.

HONORÉ DE BALZAC
FRENCH NOVELIST AND PLAYWRIGHT (1779–1850)

CONTEMPLATION

A short walk in the dark before going to bed can be a very restful thing. Above the turmoil of the world, beyond the clouds, the Moon and stars drift silently across the sky; contemplating them can relax our being into a more peaceful state of mind.

From 'THE ART OF MINDFUL SILENCE'
ADAM FORD

SIMPLY BEING

When we're drawing in nature, it's easier to move into that state of simply being. We are just there with the calmness and stillness of the natural world, and consequently become even more aware of the reach of our awareness.

From 'MINDFULNESS & THE ART OF DRAWING'
WENDY ANN GREENHALGH

ZEN SWIMMING

*As you swim, your mind may wander;
thoughts will come and go. Don't fight against
them — let the thought in, welcome it and then
leave it to one side as you regain your focus
with the next breath.*

From 'THE MINDFUL ART OF WILD SWIMMING'
TESSA WARDLEY

BODY & BREATH

Let judgements or opinions drift away like clouds in the sky. Return to your body and breath … body and breath … body and breath.

From 'MINDFULNESS & COMPASSION'
THE HAPPY BUDDHA

BE STILL

◆

Be still, my heart, these great trees are prayers.

From 'STRAY BIRDS'
RABINDRANATH TAGORE
INDIAN POET (1861–1941)

CHAPTER NINE

Our True Nature

OUR TRUE NATURE IS WHAT IS
LEFT WHEN WE STRIP AWAY THE EFFECTS
OF OUR LIFE EXPERIENCE. SPENDING TIME
MINDFULLY IN A NATURAL ENVIRONMENT
OPENS US UP TO OUR TRUE SELVES.
NATURE IS OUR SAFE PLACE.

OPENING TO THE SUN
OF COMPASSION

---

*Compassion is like the sun. We do not
need to create the sun; we simply wait until
the clouds part and the sun will shine.*

From 'MINDFULNESS & COMPASSION'
THE HAPPY BUDDHA

INTRINSIC VALUE

—◆—

Animals, insects, plants, forests, mountains, rivers as well as humans have intrinsic value. Humans have no more licence to exploit nature than they have to exploit other humans.

From 'SOIL, SOUL, SOCIETY'
SATISH KUMAR

CONNECTING

◆

A deeper connection to nature encourages

a deeper connection with our true selves.

From 'MINDFULNESS & THE NATURAL WORLD'
CLAIRE THOMPSON

FINDING REFUGE

◆

*In times of danger, we need a safe place
to return to. In times of stress, we need
solid ground to rest on.*

From 'MINDFULNESS FOR UNRAVELLING ANXIETY'
RICHARD GILPIN

TRUE WEALTH

*In classical economics, the true wealth
was land, forests, animals, minerals, rivers,
human ingenuity, creativity and skills.*

From 'SOIL, SOUL, SOCIETY'
SATISH KUMAR

SPACIOUS AWARENESS

◆

The unbounded and joyful is our true nature

and not a thing in itself. It is like the sky.

From 'MINDFULNESS & COMPASSION'
THE HAPPY BUDDHA

New Sun

◆

The sun is new each day.

HERACLITUS OF EPHESUS
GREEK PHILOSOPHER (*c.* SIXTH CENTURY BCE)

THE BODYMIND

Intuition is not a mystical state of inspiration but a hard-won state of expertise gained through practice.

From 'MINDFULNESS & SURFING'
SAM BLEAKLEY

The Beauty of Life

We can all let the magnificence of nature
touch us as we enquire deeper into its beauty.
The potential for joy in the simple delight of
appreciating natural beauty is in us
all as an end in itself.

From 'MINDFULNESS & THE NATURAL WORLD'
CLAIRE THOMPSON

WE ARE ONE

*Mindfulness and compassion are
what our planet needs — not more idealism,
but moment-to-moment mindfulness and
a trust in the goodness that lies
within us all.*

From 'MINDFULNESS & COMPASSION'
THE HAPPY BUDDHA

LIVING PEACEFULLY

♦

*Create health, beauty and permanence
and learn to live peacefully, not only with
our fellow humans but also with nature.*

From 'SOIL, SOUL, SOCIETY'
SATISH KUMAR

THERE IS TIME ENOUGH

◆

The butterfly counts not months but moments, and has time enough.

From '*I TOUCH GOD IN MY SONG*'
RABINDRANATH TAGORE
INDIAN POET (1861–1941)

LIVING MINDFULLY

WHEN WE LIVE MINDFULLY,
WE LIVE THOUGHTFULLY. WE APPRECIATE
THE BEAUTY OF OUR ENVIRONMENT AND
WE RECOGNIZE OUR PLACE IN IT.
WE DISCOVER WHAT IT IS
TO BE HAPPY.

GROWTH

Now I see the secret of the
making of the best persons,
It is to grow in the open air and
to eat and sleep with the earth.

From 'SONG OF THE OPEN ROAD'
WALT WHITMAN
AMERICAN POET (1819–92)

LIVE PURELY

———————◆———————

Meditate. Live purely. Be quiet.
Do your work with mastery. Like the moon,
come out from behind the clouds! Shine.

THE BUDDHA
(c. SIXTH CENTURY BCE)

SEEING NATURE

We do not see nature with our eyes,

but with our understandings and our hearts.

From 'THOUGHTS ON TASTE'
WILLIAM HAZLITT
ENGLISH WRITER (1778–1830)

To Be Happy

❖

In seed time learn, in harvest teach,

in winter enjoy.

From 'THE MARRIAGE OF HEAVEN AND HELL'
WILLIAM BLAKE
ENGLISH POET AND PAINTER (1757–1827)

TIME TO REST

◆

*Rest is not idleness, and to lie sometimes
on the grass under the trees on a summer's day,
listening to the murmur of water, or watching
the clouds float across the blue sky, is by no
means a waste of time.*

From 'THE USE OF LIFE'
JOHN LUBBOCK
ENGLISH SCIENTIST AND POLYMATH (1834–1913)

Beauty is Everywhere

◆

If one truly loves nature,
one finds beauty everywhere.

VINCENT VAN GOGH
DUTCH PAINTER (1853–90)

SEEDS

*All the flowers of all the tomorrows
are in the seeds of today.*

ANON

DANCE OF LIFE

---◆---

*We ought to dance with rapture that
we should be alive ... and part of the
living, incarnate cosmos.*

From 'APOCALYPSE'
D.H. LAWRENCE
ENGLISH NOVELIST (1885–1930)

ENVIRONMENT

A nation that destroys its soils destroys itself.
Forests are the lungs of our land, purifying the
air and giving fresh strength to our people.

FRANKLIN D. ROOSEVELT
32ND PRESIDENT OF THE UNITED STATES (1882-1945)

BE GLAD

---◆---

Be glad of life because it gives

you the chance to love, to work, to play,

and to look up at the stars.

HENRY VAN DYKE
AMERICAN AUTHOR AND CLERGYMAN (1852–1933)

WILD PLACES

The mind I love must still have wild
places, a tangled orchard where dark damsons
drop in the heavy grass, an overgrown little wood,
the chance of a snake or two (real snakes), a pool
that nobody's fathomed the depth of — and
paths threaded with those little flowers
planted by the mind.

From 'CULTIVATED MINDS'
KATHERINE MANSFIELD
NEW ZEALAND WRITER (1888–1923)

BEING IN NATURE

◆

Love our natural home. Spend time strolling
by the sea, swimming in lakes, sitting under trees,
walking through forests, climbing up mountains
and feeling warm sunshine and cold rain on your
face. Listen, watch, smell, touch and taste nature
all around you. Discover your favourite ways of
experiencing the natural world. May being in
nature always gift you with a sense of belonging
and inspire you to be your beautiful,
free and authentic self.

CLAIRE THOMPSON
AUTHOR OF 'MINDFULNESS & THE NATURAL WORLD'
AND 'THE ART OF MINDFUL BIRDWATCHING'

DIRECTIVE

MAY THE WORLD FORGIVE us for treating it as a possession to be exploited; may we become more mindful of the sacredness of nature, that it exists for its own sake, in its own way; and may we, by becoming more open to its beauty, learn to take deep delight in all its living forms.

The Mindfulness Series

The Art of Mindful Baking
Julia Ponsonby
ISBN: 978-1-78240-080-6

The Art of Mindful Gardening
Ark Redwood
ISBN: 978-1-907332-59-3

The Art of Mindful Silence
Adam Ford
ISBN: 978-1-908005-11-3

The Art of Mindful Singing
Jeremy Dion
ISBN: 978-1-78240-419-4

The Art of Mindful Walking
Adam Ford
ISBN: 978-1-907332-58-6

*Einstein & the Art of
Mindful Cycling*
Ben Irvine
ISBN: 978-1-908005-47-2

*Galileo & the Art of
Ageing Mindfully*
Adam Ford
ISBN: 978-1-78240-243-5

Happiness & How it Happens
The Happy Buddha
ISBN: 978-1-907332-93-7

The Heart of Mindful Relationships
Maria Arpa
ISBN: 978-1-908005-29-8

Meditation & the Art of Beekeeping
Mark Magill
ISBN: 978-1-907332-39-5

Mindfulness & Compassion
The Happy Buddha
ISBN: 978-1-78240-288-6

Mindfulness & Surfing
Sam Bleakley
ISBN: 978-1-78240-329-6

*Mindfulness & the
Art of Drawing*
Wendy Ann Greenhalgh
ISBN: 978-1-78240-283-1

*Mindfulness & the Art of
Managing Anger*
Mike Fisher
ISBN: 978-1-908005-30-4

*Mindfulness & the
Art of Urban Living*
Adam Ford
ISBN: 978-1-908005-77-9

*Mindfulness & the
Journey of Bereavement*
Peter Bridgewater
ISBN: 978-1-78240-206-0

*Mindfulness & the
Natural World*
Claire Thompson
ISBN: 978-1-78240-102-5

Mindfulness at Work
Maria Arpa
ISBN: 978-1-908005-76-2

*Mindfulness for
Black Dogs & Blue Days*
Richard Gilpin
ISBN: 978-1-907332-92-0

*Mindfulness for
Unravelling Anxiety*
Richard Gilpin
ISBN: 978-1-78240-318-0

The Mindfulness in Knitting
Rachael Matthews
ISBN: 978-1-78240-418-7

Moments of Mindfulness
ISBN: 978-1-78240-251-0

*Zen & the Art of
Raising Chickens*
Clea Danaan
ISBN: 978-1-907332-38-8

*Zen & the Path of
Mindful Parenting*
Clea Danaan
ISBN: 978-1-78240-154-4

INDEX

Anon 144

Arpa, Maria 98

de Balzac, Honoré 116

Blake, William 141

Bleakley, Sam 20, 22, 25, 27, 37,
    62, 64, 66, 79, 86, 91, 95, 97,
    102, 105, 114, 131

The Buddha 53, 83, 139

Burroughs, John 110

Byron, Lord 81

da Vinci, Leonardo 21

Dion, Jeremy 48, 99

Einstein, Albert 38, 52

Ford, Adam 69, 78, 87, 111, 117

Gandhi, Mahatma 35

Gilpin, Richard 67, 82, 127

von Goethe, Johann Wolfgang 56

Greenhalgh, Wendy Ann 34, 36, 90,
    96, 118

The Happy Buddha 28, 39, 60, 63,
    68, 77, 94, 104, 107, 120, 124,
    129, 133

Hazlitt, William 140

Heraclitus of Ephesus 80, 130

Ibsen, Henrik 24

Irvine, Ben 23

Kierkegaard, Søren 74

Kumar, Satish 33, 43, 47, 54, 85,
    115, 125, 128, 134

Lawrence, D.H. 145
Longfellow, Henry Wadsworth
   61, 70
Lubbock, John 142

Mansfield, Katherine 148
Melville, Herman 76
More, Hannah 26

Rodin, Auguste 113
Roosevelt, Franklin D. 146
Ruskin, John 41

Seattle, Chief 57
Shakespeare, William 49
Socrates 42

Tagore, Rabindranath 32, 55, 121,
   135
Thompson, Claire 8-11, 15, 46, 50,
   93, 103, 106, 126, 132, 149
Thoreau, Henry David 40
Tzu, Lao 71

Van Dyke, Henry 147
van Gogh, Vincent 143
Verne, Jules 29

Wardley, Tessa 51, 65, 75, 84, 92,
   112, 119
Whitman, Walt 138

ACKNOWLEDGEMENTS

The publisher would like to thank
Maria Arpa, Sam Bleakley, Jeremy Dion, Adam Ford,
Richard Gilpin, Wendy Ann Greenhalgh, The Happy Buddha, Ben Irvine,
Satish Kumar, Claire Thompson & Tessa Wardley.